T0198787

The Kindergarten Assistant

Chasity Williams

AuthorHouse™
1663 Liberty Drive
Bloomington, IN 47403
www.authorhouse.com
Phone: 1 (800) 839-8640

Published by AuthorHouse 08/24/2018

ISBN: 978-1-5462-5665-6 (sc)
ISBN: 978-1-5462-5666-3 (e)

Library of Congress Control Number: 2018909911

Print information available on the last page.

Any people depicted in stock imagery provided by Getty Images are models,
and such images are being used for illustrative purposes only.
Certain stock imagery © Getty Images.

This book is printed on acid-free paper.

Because of the dynamic nature of the Internet, any web addresses or links contained in this book may have changed
since publication and may no longer be valid. The views expressed in this work are solely those of the author and do not
necessarily reflect the views of the publisher, and the publisher hereby disclaims any responsibility for them.

authorHOUSE®

I dedicate this book to my Mammaw,
Emily Faye, and to my son, Ben.

"Good morning everyone!" said Ms. Williams excitedly.

"Ms. Williams, will you tie my shoe?" asks Lindsay.

"Yes Ma'am", answered Ms. Williams as she set her stuff down and kneeled to tie the shoe.

"Ms. Williams," said Andrew, "my zipper's stuck."

Ms. Williams looked at the zipper on his coat. While pulling and tugging at the zipper, the zipper popped off and flying just right, landed across the room in the fish aquarium.

Ka-plop!!!

"Oh dear!" said Ms. Williams. The kids were giggling and laughing. "We need a solution before our teacher comes back."

"Let's fish it out!" exclaimed Henry.

"Let's blow up the tank!" hollered Andrew.

"Let's pour the water out," said Lindsay grinning.

"My goodness," said Ms. Williams. "Those sound like wonderful ideas, except we must remember that for every action, there are consequences. I believe blowing up the tank and pouring the water out would hurt our pet, Sharkie, and create major messes.

"Great Circus Planes!" cried Andrew.

"I wouldn't want Sharkie to not swim good," said Lindsay with a worried look on her face.

"Don't worry Lindsay," said Ms. Williams, "Sharkie is safe."

"Look!" exclaimed Sammy, "Sharkie's playing with the zipper!"

While the students giggled, Ms. Williams took action and began digging in the boxes in the science corner of the classroom.

"Where is it?" asks Ms. Williams. "There it is!" Walking back with a string and a tangerine size magnet.

"Awesome Ms. Williams!" exclaimed Henry. "We're gonna do my fishing idea!"

"Right you are, Henry," said Ms. Williams. "We need Mrs. Morgan's long ruler." Sammy brought the long ruler from the chalk board.

The strings were tied. One end on the magnet and the other end on the long ruler.

"Great Hold–gie Ba–tacks!!!" exclaimed Ms. Williams! Using her son's favorite saying when he wanted super hugs. Ben always loves his super hugs!

Giggles followed with puzzled looks from the students.

"Sharkie is jumping out of the aquarium!" cried Ms. Williams as she jumped over surrounding desks trying to catch the flying pet.

"Ms. Williams!" exclaimed Mrs. Morgan.

"What on earth!" exclaimed the principal, Mrs. Gilliam.

As desks flipped over and chairs scooted.

"I caught him!" yelled Ms. Williams, lying flat on her back with both hands on the tail whipping baby hammerhead shark known to everyone as Sharkie.

"Great news," said Andrew, "I got my zipper back! It fell out of Sharkie's mouth. Thank you, Ms. Williams. Thank you so much!"

"Anytime sweetie," said Ms. Williams as she easily set Sharkie back in the aquarium.

"Time to close the lid on this wanna be airplane!"

"You saved Sharkie's life!" exclaimed Lindsay, "Ms. Williams, number 10 is no longer my hero, you are!!!" The students started hugging Ms. Williams.

"Remember students" said Ms. Williams, "for every action, whether good or bad, there are always consequences."

"Ms. Williams, please come to my office, now!" said the principal in a very unhappy tone.

In the principal's office, Mrs. Gilliam explained the safety rules to Ms. Williams again for the 4th time.

"Yes Ma'am," replied Ms. Williams, "I will be more careful."

"You are excused to go back to your room," said the principal.

"Thank you, Ma'am," said Ms. Williams.

Later at lunch...

"Ms. Williams," cried Emily, "my zipper's stuck!"

"Oh dear," said a very worried Ms. Williams, "here we go again. I wonder where this zipper will land."

"Ms. Williams!" hollered Mrs. Morgan, "This zipper landed right in my bowl of chili!"

Hearing giggles from surrounding students, Ms. Williams thought, I'm gonna be the 1st kindergarten assistant to receive detention.

And so, she did. Plus, writing 100 times: I will be respectful, responsible and kind, and leave zippers alone.

The End

Hi youngsters! Please fill free to be creative! You may draw your very own "Sharkie" or classroom pet.

Don't ever give up! You may draw your very own "number 10 super hero".

Let those imaginations soar! You may draw "circus planes".

Be brave! You may draw your very own "teacher".

Be spontaneous! You may draw your very own "popping zipper".

Run like the wind! You may draw your very own "aquarium". I wonder what animals you will put inside your aquarium.

Last but not least, please be respectful, responsible, and kind to others. You may draw and write your very own "rules of the classroom".

Printed in the United States
By Bookmasters